TOXIC CHARACTER TYPES

How to Let Go
How to Thrive
How to Find The Emotional Freedom You Deserve

ZEELAH S. DAVIS

Published by:

ISBN: 978-1-958404-79-9 (paperback)

DEDICATION

This book is dedicated to my one daughter, Justine, who, without even knowing it, pushed me to remain grounded while writing this book. After the third edits of this book, I found comfort as the idea of the cartoon caricature depictions surfaced.

ACKNOWLEDGMENTS

I want to acknowledge my oldest brother, Danvas Atkinson, for his invaluable impact that challenged me to see beyond the surface in my growth and understanding. He pushed me to delve deeper, to question not just words but actions, and to seek out relevant inquiries that opened up new doors of insight and introspection. His constant encouragement to explore beneath the obvious not only broadened my perspective but also encouraged me to think critically and authentically.

TABLE OF CONTENTS

CHAPTER 1

THE ROCKET

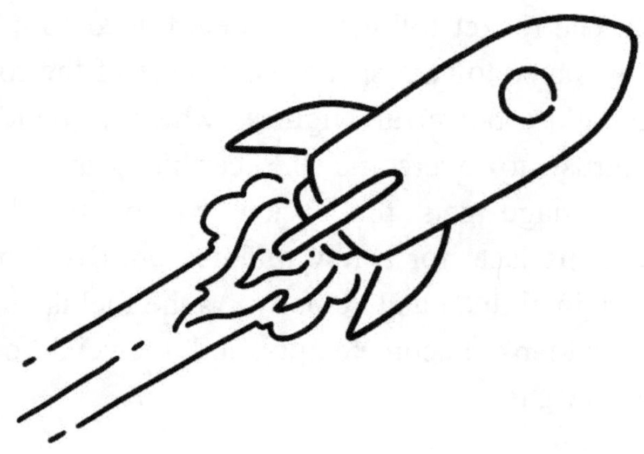

While reflecting on the life we live, two aspects always jump out at me: the adjustments and changes that we have to make that are considered to be external and the changes we undergo within ourselves that are considered to be internal. These two aspects—external and internal—are reminiscent of the story of the rocket and the story of a tree that I find intriguing. I will give an account of both below and I hope you can expand your understanding to think about your life the same way.

There is an account of a rocket on its path to escape the confines of earth into the deep, vast promises of outer space. There are three stages for the rocket to travel into space on this path of escape.

In the first phase, liftoff and ascent, the engines of the rocket are fired up to provide the necessary thrust to lift the rocket from the launch pad and accelerate it into the earth's atmosphere. The rocket follows a predetermined path as it maintains its course toward space. This stage of the rocket contains the most powerful engines, which provide the necessary thrust to overcome the earth's gravity. The rocket's first stage gets the rocket out of the lower atmosphere. This lasts for a few minutes until the rocket reaches a certain altitude and velocity. As the fuel is burned off, the external tanks become empty, and the weight of the rocket is much lighter.

The second phase is called the cruise stage. Once the rocket reaches the desired altitude and velocity, it discards the empty fuel canisters to prolong the flight. The empty tanks fall back to earth. The rocket continues on its planned trajectory, with its engines firing periodically to maintain speed and height. During this stage, the rocket usually travels above the earth's atmosphere and into space.

The third stage, called payload separation, is the final stage. In the final stage, the rocket enters its designated orbit around the earth. The rocket's engines are again fired to adjust the direction, speed, and altitude of the orbit. After the rocket reaches its designated orbit, the payload will be separated from the rocket. The payload includes the spacecraft, satellites, or other equipment that will travel in space to perform various activities.

The actual sequence and duration of each stage might vary depending on the type of rocket, its mission, and other factors.

One of the key points to note in the rocket's travel from earth to outer space is that to lighten the weight of the vehicle to achieve its designated orbit, most rockets discard a portion of the vehicle at the end of stages 1 and 2. It is physically impossible to carry the discarded material into the next stage as this could put the rocket at risk and jeopardize the success of the launch.

Frankly, the rockets have to discard what needs to be discarded at each stage before they can move to a higher altitude. So it is on our life journey; there comes a time when we too have to eject people from our lives as we manoeuvre through the various iterations of moving up in age and stage of our lives.

The person that you went to primary school with is not necessarily the person you will retire with. The person you went to high school with may not be the best man at your wedding.

The thought of having to separate yourself from others as you move to another stage in life does not only occur on your side; others may have to separate themselves from you also. Have you ever wondered why that person you were such good friends with just stopped talking to you? They stop returning your calls and never seem to have time for your monthly link-up. News flash: they have moved on!

THE TREE

A similar comparison can be made when you look at the problems that can develop when a tree is not pruned regularly.

When a tree is not pruned regularly, overgrown branches can crowd out other branches, leading to stunted growth and creating safety hazards.

Dead, diseased or damaged branches, when left unattended, can spread disease to other parts of the tree.

A non-pruned tree can have a lopsided appearance or awkward branching, affecting the overall looks of the tree.

Fruits and flowers require sunlight to grow and develop. An unpruned tree will have a greater number of branches that block sunlight, which may hamper fruit or flower production.

Unpruned trees tend to carry excess weight, which may cause branches to break apart during high winds and precipitation events.

In summary, a lack of pruning can have detrimental effects on the growth, health, and overall appearance of a tree. Therefore, to maintain a healthy and attractive tree, it is advisable to prune it regularly.

We all have our individual goals and aspirations in life and not everyone will understand, appreciate, and support our mission. Having these people around can hinder your progress and crowd out the vision you have, resulting in stunted growth. Often times, these persons are unwilling to change their pattern of living, and keeping them around too long will have a negative impact on you. It's as if their expiration time has been reached and we are too afraid to let them go. You are your own self-preservation, and these people need to be pruned.

He who walks with wise men will be wise, but the companion of fools will be destroyed. (Proverbs 13:20 – NKJV).

But understand this, that in the last days there will come times of difficulty. For people will be lovers of self, lovers of money, proud, arrogant, abusive, disobedient to their parents, ungrateful, unholy, heartless, unappeasable, slanderous, without self-control, brutal, not loving good, treacherous, reckless, swollen with conceit, lovers of pleasure rather than lovers of God, having the appearance of godliness, but denying its power. Avoid such people. (2 Timothy 3:1-5 – ESV).

My overall thought on being free from toxic individuals is that we need to gain an appreciation of the various aspects of toxicity and open our minds to things that we have perhaps missed. You may also have resigned yourself to self-doubt, feeling it was all in your head and casting blame on yourself, and this should not be how it goes. The truth is, toxic people are everywhere we go, and as unfortunate as we may feel, we have no choice but to interact with them daily.

Some experts have concluded that toxic people are generally narcissistic. I, however, will leave the classification to these experts to propagate as I consider this to be a God-given right they have earned based on the training path they have undergone. I, being a mere mortal, only get the privilege of highlighting the toxic behaviors I have encountered that have forcefully led me to the conclusion that there is a need to be free from them lest I suffer their venom or end up being beguiled to join the leader's toxic pack. Shane Parish, who is described by Business Insider as 'Wall Street's biggest influencer' puts it like this, *"Distance yourself from people you don't want to become."*

CHAPTER 2

WHY DID I BECOME INTERESTED IN THIS TOPIC

It all started when I met with Sally. Sally is someone I had known for years. Sally was now a medical doctor. We both attended the same church as teenagers, and we also went to the same university. We pursued different areas of study, of course. We had been out of touch for years, and we met up at a surprise birthday party I was having for my son, who was now twenty years old. The surprising news she told me was that her parents were no longer together. They first separated and were now divorced. They had been married for over forty years. In the end, her mom said her dad was a toxic narcissist, and she could not go on any longer being married or sharing the same space with him. This story was like the straw that broke the camel's back for me. I felt like I kept hearing the word "toxic" in almost every conversation I heard, more so on social media. It was now to the point where I think it had become normalized.

The story of Sally's parents is not an isolated event. I have heard many stories involving families and friendships that were destroyed by toxic name-calling and characterization that seem to be raft with ignorance due to a lack of knowledge, where people just repeat what they hear.

But, do we really know what it means to be toxic? That was my question to myself, so I decided then and there that I would go on a mission to uncover the true meaning of the pronouncement of being toxic and toxic characterization. My plan was never to be selfish in my findings but to share what I have discovered with others so they can be illuminated with this knowledge. Hopefully, this would put an end to, or at least result in a fall in, the number of families being destroyed.

What I have outlined in this book are but a few of the toxic characters I uncovered that I think we all need to understand. I have also included the importance of doing an evaluation of ourselves to determine if we fall guilty to any of these characteristics.

I think renowned author, Robert Greene, masterfully captures the consequences of someone who ignores the need to systematically observe and analyze their thoughts, values, and actions when he states, *"There is no one more dangerous than a person who has no self-awareness. They can't see who they are because that gives them license to do whatever they want and feel justified."*

With all the advances we have seen in life, the one thing that always remains the same is that people want power and control. Quite often, people don't care about your feelings when they attain this power, and if you are a pushover, they will roll over you.

We need to reach the point of realizing that we alone are responsible for our own well-being and happiness. You deserve to be treated properly. You matter. Your feelings and emotions matter. Your thoughts and perspective matter. You deserve respect. You should not always have to be adjusting to others and situations to fit in.

Stop being a pushover!

CHAPTER 3

DETECTING TOXIC PEOPLE

People wear masks, and masks camouflage them from showing their true identity and what is going on in their life because, in so doing, others can't reject them for who they truly are. We should not expect that the true essence of someone's character will be like an armband worn in full display. Arthur Schopenhauer, a German philosopher, when talking about how people learn to disguise themselves, says, *"You will always be the prey or*

the plaything of the devils and fools in this world if you expect to see them going about with horns or jangling their bells."

The reality is that we may presently have people in our lives that are toxic. They could be our romantic partner, people we work with or maybe a close friend. Toxic behavior in people can stem from a variety of reasons, such as past experiences, insecurities or learned behaviors. Some toxic individuals can be very cunning and crafty. They exhibit these behaviors as a defence mechanism or as a way to manipulate others to meet their own needs.

An article by WebMD editorial contributors says, *"If you know someone who's difficult and causes a lot of conflict in your life, you may be dealing with a toxic person. It went on to say that these people can create lots of stress and unpleasantness for you and others, not to mention emotional or even physical pain."*

Detecting toxic people can be beneficial for your mental and emotional well-being. By recognizing toxic behaviors and relationships, you can make informed decisions about who to surround yourself with. This can help you maintain positive energy, reduce stress, and protect yourself from harm or unhealthy influences. Additionally, learning to set boundaries with toxic individuals can lead to healthier and more fulfilling relationships.

Detecting toxic people can sometimes be challenging because we often take appearance for reality, and we judge others by their appearances and the image they project through their actions and words. Frankly, by trusting the very appearance of someone, you have already limited yourself to uncovering the true character of others.

Below are some warnings for detecting toxic people. Let this be a guide on what to look out for if you think you are dealing with a toxic person. I have deliberately not made this list long and drawn out but as short as possible so it can be easily understood and easily remembered. It may even be beneficial to memorize this list:

1. They are always negative and constantly complain. They may also try to bring you down with their negativity.

2. They consistently criticize and belittle you or others around them.

3. They may appear friendly at first, but soon, their behavior becomes manipulative, controlling, and selfish.

4. They lack empathy and may disregard the feelings and needs of others.

5. They are charming and always want to be the center of attention, and often make conversations about themselves.

6. They may try to isolate you from your friends and family or discourage you from pursuing your goals.

7. They may have a history of failed relationships and conflicts with others.

Let us not be too quick, however, to classify persons by ticking through the list provided above. There should be a consistent display of these characteristics over an observed period of time. If this is who they are, they will be consistent in how they operate, and that is when you need to take action to separate yourself from them. Release the attachments you have with them. Move on to embracing freedom and finding inner peace.

CHAPTER 4

PEOPLE WHO GOSSIP

Gossiping is one of the characteristics displayed by toxic individuals that you need to watch out for. Gossip can lead to the spread of false information, which can damage a person's reputation and lead to misunderstandings and conflicts. It can also create a toxic and negative environment, leading to decreased trust and morale within a community.

According to pastor Matt Mitchell of Lane, Pennsylvania, gossip hurts neighbors, divide friends, and damages reputations and relationships. This statement is also confirmed in Romans 1:29, which states: *"They were filled with all manner of unrighteousness, evil, covetousness, and malice. They are full of envy, murder, strife, deceit, and maliciousness. They are gossips." (ESV).*

This scripture, without a doubt, confirms the toxic nature of those who gossip and the toxic effects of the gossip they perpetrate, which are envy, murder, strife, deceit, and maliciousness. These are considered to be the results of a depraved mind. There is a great quote that I heard, and I can't remember who said it, but it goes like this: "**Small minds discuss other people**." It's as if they are in control and they are the trusted source of information and, more precisely, the source of people's business.

Gossipers will do anything to earn your trust so you drop your guard and feel comfortable sharing personal and sensitive details with them. Having your information, they become emboldened, and no sooner you are not in their presence, they begin to share this information with others. This somehow shows that they are a part of your inner circle and have power over you. People who gossip are always studying you and looking for weaknesses that they can share with others.

Avoiding people who gossip can be beneficial for several reasons. Gossip can indeed damage relationships by spreading misinformation, causing misunderstandings, and ultimately leading to conflicts. When you surround yourself with people who gossip, you may risk being dragged into drama, becoming the subject of gossip yourself or being exposed to a negative and toxic environment.

Additionally, encountering people who gossip can have other negative effects, such as erosion of trust, loss of credibility, increased anxiety or stress, and an overall decrease in morale. It can also create a toxic culture where speaking ill of others behind their backs become normalized, leading to a lack of authentic and healthy communication among people.

It is important to be mindful of the company you keep and to prioritize building relationships with individuals who value open and honest communication, respect boundaries, and focus on uplifting and supporting each other rather than tearing others down through gossip.

There is a quote I heard on TikTok. I am not sure of its source but I think it is important to always keep it in mind when it comes to people who gossip. It goes like this, *"When people hear good things about you, they stay silent. When they hear bad things about you, they spread it like wildfire. But when they hear nothing about you, they make things up. However, it's important to remember that you cannot control what people say or what they do."*

CHAPTER 5

POWER AND MANIPULATION

I would like to start this chapter by recognizing the fact that everyone needs power. People often seek power because it allows them to have control over their own lives and the ability to influence the world around them.

A famous quote by Robert Shenkkan says, *"Everybody wants power. Everybody. And if they say they don't, they're lying."*

Throughout history, and across various societies, the desire for power and control has been a recurring theme. One could argue that this desire is ingrained in human nature, evident in the pursuit of dominance, influence, and authority in personal, social, and political contexts. Philosophers like Thomas Hobbes suggested that power struggles are inevitable due to human nature's inclination toward self-preservation and competitiveness. This drive for power and control has led to conflicts, wars, and hierarchies in various human constructs. Even in modern times, advancements in technology, economy, and culture have not eradicated this basic human drive for power and control, as seen in interpersonal relationships, corporate power struggles, and political machinations. This relentless quest for power and control seems to be a fundamental aspect of human behavior that persists despite societal advancements.

It is important, however, to remember that power should be used responsibly and for the greater good of all rather than for selfish purposes. Where power becomes toxic is when it is used for selfish purposes, more so with the view of manipulating others. Toxic people love to manipulate those around them to get what they want. They will lie, bend the truth, exaggerate, or even leave out critical information so that you have a certain opinion of them. They will go to lengths to use tactics to conceal their true intention. They will do pretty much whatever it takes, even if it means hurting you.

Manipulators stay on point and message. They will tell you the same story all day, every day. They are very consistent. It is like a gentle program that systematically runs through your head, over and over, until you start believing that this is your own thought, and this thought you are having reflects the truth. Tell me one person who will not trust their own thought.

A new study by the University of Konstanz in July 2020 finds that groups led by subordinate males outperform those led by dominant and aggressive males. Yes, groups led by manipulators and those hungry for power never perform at their optimal.

Manipulators bring everyone down because of envy. In their minds, they are at the top, but the reality is that they are tearing down people above them to pull them down to their level. According to Andrew Tate, *"Hate never comes from above, it comes from below."*

Here are a few signs that someone is manipulating you:

1. They know your weaknesses and how to exploit them.
2. They use your insecurities against you.
3. They convince you to give up something important to you to make you more dependent on them.
4. If they succeed in their manipulation, they will continue to do so until you get out of the situation.

They will manipulate you unless you know their techniques.

On the opposite side of power and manipulation is a corporative partnership; people working or acting together willingly for a common purpose or benefit. There is power in partnership when you have the right people around you who can lift you when you fall, who will catch you before you fall, who can see danger coming and warn you ahead of time, and who can just be downright real with you.

CHAPTER 6

THE BULLY

Because we think we encountered bullies so long ago in our past life, you might be asking "Who is a bully?" Well, a bully is a person who habitually seeks to harm or intimidate those whom they perceive as vulnerable. Now that you have been reminded of this, it is now clear to see that the same bullies you encountered as a child are the same bullies you are now encountering as an adult. It will therefore be no surprise that researchers have found that bullying lingers well into adulthood and follows you into the workplace. This has given rise to terms like workplace bullies and also adult bullies. Bullies were not only in primary school, and bullies can be at any age. Bullies can be your boss at work and can be your team members.

Bullies fall into the category of mean people, and mean people don't just stop being mean. Similarly, it is not expected that by some magic as soon as bullies graduate from primary school, they just stop being bullies.

Bullies need people to be subservient to them. They put people down so they can feel like they are up. They use deliberate, aggressive attempts against a weak individual to cause harm. Adult bullies want to control and take advantage of you. No wonder in primary school, bullies look out for someone who is smaller than them, and in their adult and work lives, they look for persons who are timid and can't speak up for themselves. In the workplace, a bully will use the knowledge they have of a particular area of work and try to belittle you to the point where you don't share your opinions because you feel downright stupid in comparison to them.

Bullying sucks your confidence!

Victims of bullying are at risk for psychiatric problems such as anxiety, depression, substance abuse, and suicide when they become adults, reported a study partially funded by the

National Institute of Mental Health (NIMH) that was published in the April issue of JAMA Psychiatry.

I wish I could detail five steps you can take to rectify the situation with a bully, but based on my research, the effects of bullying can be complex and are best dealt with under the guidance of a trained professional capable of handling it.

Here are some signs to look for to know if you are dealing with a bully and need to seek attention:

- If you somehow feel unease in the presence of someone who you suspect is a bully, then seek help.

- If you dread workplace meetings that involve a particular individual that sends chills and causes you anxiety, then seek help.

- If you have difficulty saying no where the thought is that people will not like you, think less of you or have a different perception of you if you say no, then seek help.

- If you feel incapable and always need external validation to give you that feel-good factor, then seek help.

Be mindful, however, that it is quite normal to seek validation around the persons you trust, such as family and those in your inner circle. These are the persons who will keep you grounded and help you determine if you are on the right path. I often ask my wife and children for feedback whenever I do something at church, and this is to determine if the intended message that I wanted to transmit was delivered.

There may be a common belief that fighting back is the best option against a bully, but the experts advise that fighting back is the best and worst thing you can do. If you fight back, they will either leave you alone and move to the next victim or dig their heels in and employ more aggressive or harder strategies to show what they are capable of and that you should not mess with them.

Here are a few practical steps you can take to address the situation:

1. Stay Calm: It is important to try to stay calm and not let the bully see that they are getting to you. Bullies often look for a reaction, so staying composed can help.

2. Seek Support: Talk to someone you trust about what is happening. This could be a teacher, school counsellor, parent or another adult who can offer guidance and support. It is important not to keep it to yourself.

3. Document the Incidents: Keep a record of the bullying incidents, including what happened, when

and where it occurred, and who was involved. This information can be helpful if you need to report the bullying.

4. Report the Bullying: If the bullying is happening at school, report it to a teacher, counsellor or principal. If the bullying is happening online or outside of school, consider reporting it to the appropriate authorities or using available reporting tools on social media platforms.

5. Build Confidence: Work on building your self-confidence and self-esteem. Engage in activities that make you feel good about yourself and surround yourself with supportive friends and family.

6. Seek Professional Help: If the bullying is causing you significant distress, consider talking to a mental health professional who can provide support and guidance.

Remember, no one deserves to be bullied, and it is important to take steps to address the situation and get the support you need.

Let me address one piece of misinformation before we complete the topic of bullies, and that is bullying behavior can be exhibited by people of any gender, and that it is important to address and confront bullying behavior regardless of who is displaying it. If you or someone you know is experiencing bullying, it is important to seek support and help from trusted individuals or professionals.

Women are bullies as well!

CHAPTER 7

AGREEABLE VERSUS DIS-AGREEABLE

Jordan Peterson, in the piece, *Perils of Being Overly Nice*, highlights that the majority of disagreeable persons are men and the majority of agreeable persons are women.

Agreeableness is a tendency to be compassionate and cooperative rather than suspicious and antagonistic towards others. The trait reflects individual differences in general concern for social harmony. Agreeable individuals value getting along with others. They are generally considerate, friendly, generous, helpful, and willing to compromise their interests with others. Agreeable people also have an optimistic view of human nature. They believe people are honest, decent, and trustworthy.

Disagreeable individuals, however, place self-interest above getting along with others. They are generally unconcerned with others' well-being and less likely to extend themselves to others. Sometimes, their skepticism about others' motives causes them to be suspicious, unfriendly, and uncooperative.

Listed below are some character traits that will help you easily identify agreeable versus disagreeable individuals:

AGREEABLE TRAITS

- I am interested in people.
- I sympathize with others' feelings.
- I have a soft heart.
- I take time out for others.
- I feel others' emotions.
- I make people feel at ease.

DISAGREEABLE TRAITS

- I am not really interested in others.
- I insult people.
- I am not interested in other people's problems.

- I feel little concern for others.
- Employs bullying tactics.[1]

While the verdict is out on whether being agreeable is best or being disagreeable is best, a research co-authored by University of Notre Dame Management, Professor Timothy Judge, titled, *Do Nice Guys and Gals Really Finish Last*, shows a strong negative relationship between agreeableness and earnings for men. The more agreeable a man is, the less he will earn, while the more disagreeable he is, the higher his earnings. But while men benefit from being disagreeable, women don't. If you are a disagreeable man, you are considered a strong negotiator. While the perception is that if a woman is agreeable, she is taken advantage of, and if she is disagreeable, she is considered a control freak.

Another paper done by Cameron Anderson, Daron L. Sharps, Christopher J. Soto, and Oliver P. John, Edited by Susan T. Fiske, Princeton University, shows that disagreeable individuals were intimidating, which would have elevated their power, but they also had poor interpersonal relationships at work, which offset any possible power advantage their behavior might have provided. In the end, being disagreeable becomes an impediment to their growth.

The main downside of this personality trait is that it never challenges the status quo. It never challenges traditional

[1] The "Big 5" Personality Traits - Crowe Associates Ltd.

ideas or old concepts—and, consequently, it rarely promotes innovation.

On the other hand, innovation is born as a result of disagreeing with the given norms. The world's most famous and successful entrepreneurs, like Thomas Edison, Steve Jobs, and other highly successful leaders, had disagreeable personalities.[2]

Is it better to be agreeable or disagreeable?

Like most traits, agreeableness is normally distributed, so most of us fall in the middle—we can be very nice at times, but we can also be somewhat disagreeable. At the low end of the agreeableness, we have people who simply aren't very nice.

It is time for you to decide:

- Am I agreeable? Should I be agreeable?
- Am I disagreeable? Should I be disagreeable?
- Should I fall in the middle, or do I fall in the middle?

It is your choice to make. However, I would recommend you seek to fall in the middle if you are not already there. Do so and give yourself a high five.

---

[2] David and Goliath: Underdogs, Misfits, and the Art of Battling Giants, Malcolm Gladwell

CHAPTER 8

NEGATIVE EMOTIONS

I had this chapter in my book outline, and in the end, I could have just not included it. However, I decided to leave it with just one line of detail on this topic. The picture I had commissioned was so prescriptive and made it even clearer that just one line would be sufficient. So here we go:

Some describe negative emotions as a war against yourself that spills over to a war against everyone else.

CHAPTER 9

POSITIVE EMOTIONS

I read somewhere that the first rule of firearm safety is to always conduct yourself in a mature and responsible manner. No wonder when you hear of people who commit atrocities like school shootings, they do so without a thought of the consequences of their actions. Most of the time, these perpetrators have higher than normal IQs but tend to act purely through emotions.

Having a high IQ does not mean your perception of and ability to recognize and act in a manner that shows your ability to differentiate between right and wrong is intact. It does not mean you have a moral compass guided by a belief system of truth, and this is why they lack positive emotions.

There is a clear difference between intelligence quotient (IQ) and emotional quotient (EQ). People with a higher EQ tend to be the persons who take into consideration the consequences of their actions and also recognize the alternate choices they have that can bring about an amicable solution rather than one that results in harm to others. They tend to talk it out or walk it out.

While IQ (Intelligence Quotient) is a measure of your ability to solve problems and think logically, EQ (Emotional Intelligence Quotient) measures your ability to understand and manage emotions. Your EQ can have a greater influence on your success in life than your IQ.

It is MY BELIEF, and I say it loudly: it is my belief based on my observation and what I have garnered from pulling on the views of some therapists that I have studied that everyone needs to possess some level of stoicism. Some people will not agree with this, particularly because this lifestyle was adopted by the very controversial Tate brothers, Andrew and Tristan Tate. These gentlemen because of their overall views on masculinity and somewhat toxic masculinity I may add, have resulted in well-thinking persons dismissing the idea and possible benefits of being stoic merely because stoicism is embraced by them.

A stoic person is one who can endure pain or hardship without showing their feelings or complaining. Stoicism is a life philosophy that emphasizes mental toughness and self-discipline as tools for living a good life. The stoic attitude is being strict with yourself and patient with others to keep your mind clear and not let negativity get to you.

The stoics have a concept somewhat like emotional intelligence; the potential for a human being to regulate their emotional responses not only to the outside world but also to our inner world, and it is this aspect that I believe fosters positive emotions guided by emotional intelligence, and this prevents one from sliding into toxicity.

Some people tend to avoid all levels of discomfort in their lives, not recognizing that discomfort is how we grow and how we become strong. This is where you decide what to change and what not to change, which is the picture of stoicism. This reminds me of when I was a teenager. I was always fascinated by martial arts or karate (as some loosely calls it), even though I am sure there is a marked distinction between them. I often watched those old Chinese movies and tried to pattern all those cool moves and imagined beating everyone who would ever cross me. To my surprise, however, when I enrolled as a student in a Karate artform called Zen Do Ki Kan, one of the first things I was told was Karate was not about fighting. It was about restraint and the inculcation of discipline as an individual. It is about knowing what you are capable of doing but deciding instead to seek peace at all cost, deciding to use your skills of self-defence as a last resort when that is the only choice you have.

Jordan Peterson, renowned Canadian therapist and author, says it like this: *"The hero has to be a monster. But a controlled monster."* People need to make themselves competent and dangerous. The alternative to this is being weak, and weak is not good. On the point I raised above about people who shoot up high schools, he says they are weak, and they lack the capacity to be controlled in their actions.

There are two paths before you; you may take only one path. One doorway is narrow. And one door is wide. Go through the narrow door. For the wide door leads to a wide path, and the wide path is broad; the wide, broad path is easy, and the wide, broad, easy path has many, many people on it; but the wide, broad, easy, crowded path leads to death. Now then that narrow door leads to a narrow road that in turn leads to life. It is hard to find that road. Not many people manage it. (Matthew 7:13-14 – The Voice).

It is up to you to choose whether you seek positive emotions or negative emotions. The choice cannot be both, but only one, and my suggestion is to choose to embrace positive emotions with its high emotional quotient (EQ), self-control, discipline, and clear directions to a mentally healthy lifestyle.

CHAPTER 10

HEALTHY RELATIONSHIPS

I have seen ladies, like my friend Linda (not her real name), who present themselves with black eyes, slashed lips, and several bruises all over their bodies. It is obvious to all what happened. In the case of Linda, she and her partner were in a constant battle. It seems they have never had a good day since they were together. Often, when asked the question if she reported this abuse to the authorities, she would quickly say "Not yet" while mumbling under her breath that she didn't want her partner to get into any entanglement with the law. This is certainly a mystery to me as it does not add up. Linda would go as far as to say that it is because her partner loves and cares for her that he does what he does. This is a contradiction, and I could never understand what would cause someone who is abused to hand over their rights to the perpetrator and tag them as the victim instead. I guess it is true the statement that says toxic people play the victim very well. No doubt, her partner had sold this story over and over to her, and she now believed it. People with a victim mentality blame others for the level of difficulty and unhappiness they have in their lives, and they think that meeting out violence to others is a way of getting justice for themselves as some sort of therapy.

The converse on women abusing men is also a reality, although not prevalent, or maybe it is not advertised as much due to stigmas of society that call men who get beaten by their partners soft and not a real man. No matter how we look at it, both of these cases are toxic, and you need to distance yourself from people who seek to abuse you like this. This is certainly not a healthy relationship.

A healthy relationship can provide numerous benefits, including a loving, supportive, and caring environment that allows partners to turn to each other for emotional support during difficult times.

Being in a healthy relationship can help reduce the risk of depression, anxiety, and other mental health concerns.

Individuals in healthy relationships tend to have better physical health, as they are more likely to engage in healthy habits such as exercising, eating healthy, and going to the doctor regularly.

Being in a healthy relationship can help improve communication skills as partners learn to communicate effectively with each other.

A healthy relationship can bring financial security, as partners may pool resources, share expenses, and support each other in their career goals.

A healthy relationship can provide a strong social support system, giving couples a network of friends and family to turn to.

Overall, a healthy relationship can provide many benefits that contribute to a happy and fulfilling life.

My parents were married for over fifty years before my father passed on in his early 90s. I remember my oldest brother, who is in his 70s, remarking that he has never seen or heard my parents argue in all his years of living with them. I would be naive to think that my parents never argued, but I think they were deliberate in making sure that this was not a staple for the ears of anyone but themselves. This is something that I found remarkable, and I have adopted this in my marriage as well. I think my wife and I have been successful at this, but my giveaway is that I go into silent mode whenever we have a misunderstanding, and my children have learned to pick up on this so well over the twenty-five years we have been married. I can almost hear them now rhetorically asking me at one of those awkward moments asking, *"Daddy, is everything okay?"* At that point, I have no option but to snap out of it, using my words very thrifty in responding, *"Yes, I am okay. Thanks for asking."*

Children are so perceptive and impressionable, and we have to be deliberate in our actions to model being a positive example to them so they can receive this in their lives and future. Sometimes, we overlook how much our children look up to us and even how much of a role model we are to them. They are like little sponges and quickly soak up the characters we display. So, if we want to mold them positively, then being intentional in our actions is the way to go.

Train up a child in the way he should go: and when he is old, he will not depart from it. (Proverbs 22:6 – KJV).

Here are fifteen red flags to look for in a relationship that are signs it is not a healthy relationship:

1. Overly controlling behavior.
2. Lack of trust.
3. Feeling low self-esteem.
4. Physical, emotional or mental abuse.
5. Substance abuse.

6. Narcissism.
7. Anger management issues.
8. Co-dependency.
9. Inability to resolve conflict.
10. Constant jealousy.
11. Gaslighting.
12. Lack of emotional intelligence.
13. Negatively affecting your relationship with family and friends.
14. Inability to communicate openly.
15. Lack of social connection or friends.

CHAPTER 11

THE EMOTIONALLY UNHEALTHY WOMAN

The emotionally unhealthy woman is a type of toxicity that I will not speak much about. I personally have never met anyone like this and I hope to God my path will never cross with one.

According to relationship coach, Sadia Khan, this type of toxicity is something that men underestimate when they are looking for a suitable partner. Men do not trust feelings, they trust facts, and in doing so, they tend to look for whoever they like. Their connection to a potential partner is purely based on physical appearance, and they often overlook all the red flags on display. They are somehow beguiled by beauty, and they think they can change a woman if they treat her well, court her correctly, and offer her the firmest, solid, steady, and secure relationship there is to be found in this world or beyond the stars to make her all his. Red flag: You can't change someone who does not want to change.

Be wary of these persons and don't ever ignore the red flags!

It is said that most women can't recognize a good man even when he is standing in front of them. The majority of abuse happens to women, and they end up building high emotional walls as they have been hurt so much, and the wall has become their de facto defence mechanism to shield every possible advance that may come their way. This does not mean she is a bad person, and neither am I suggesting this, but her past hurt has made her hard to open up to anyone. If she is willing to open her eyes and heart, she could actually have the man of your dreams.

I could not end this chapter and not also talk about toxic men, lest you think I am crying blame on the woman and forgetting the involvement of men altogether. Let me say unequivocally that, yes, there are toxic men too; men who are damaged and dangerous, whose actions are not detectable when you first meet them. They start out with great chemistry but become the monster that brings horror and trauma over time. This is why it is important not to ignore red flags. One good method of uncovering their hidden character is to ensure as much as possible to be in the same space with them and their sibling, particularly their sister or mother. It is very likely that the way they treat their sister and mother is the same way they will treat you. This is not a foolproof method, however, particularly when it comes to the relationship between them and their mother. In some cases, no one is more important to them than their mother, and you will always play second fiddle. Anything you do is wrong in their eyes, but their mother can do no harm.

CHAPTER 12

THE GASLIGHTER

A gaslighter is a person who uses psychological methods to manipulate someone into questioning their own sanity or power of reasoning.

Gaslighting is a manipulative tactic in which a person, to gain power and control of another individual, plants seeds of uncertainty in another person's mind. The self-doubt and constant questioning slowly cause the individual to question their reality.

Signs of gaslighting:

1. Insisting you said or did things you know you didn't do.
2. Denying or scoffing at your recollection of events.
3. Calling you "too sensitive" or "crazy" when you express your needs or concerns.
4. Expressing doubts to others about your feelings, behavior, and state of mind.
5. Twisting or retelling events to shift blame to you.

Experiencing gaslighting can leave you second-guessing yourself constantly, not to mention overwhelmed, confused, and uncertain about your ability to make decisions on your own.

Other key signs you are experiencing gaslighting include:

1. An urge to apologize all the time.
2. Believing you can't do anything right.
3. Frequent feelings of nervousness, anxiety, or worry.
4. A loss of confidence.
5. Constantly wondering if you're too sensitive.
6. Feeling disconnected from your sense of self, as if you're losing your identity.

7. Believing you're to blame when things go wrong.
8. A persistent sense that something isn't right, though you can't identify exactly what is wrong.
9. A lingering sense of hopelessness, frustration, or emotional numbness.

Over time, gaslighting can affect your sense of self-worth, leave you unsure about making decisions, and contribute to feelings of anxiety, depression, and loneliness.[3]

HOW TO DEAL WITH GASLIGHTING

Stand firm in your truth: That means believing in yourself, your feelings, and what you know to be true. It means owning your perception (i.e., what you saw, heard, and felt). It sounds like, "I know what I saw" or "Don't tell me how to feel; this is how I feel."

Be willing to leave the conversation: The goal of the person who is gaslighting is to have you doubt your perception, so walking away before the gaslighting gets severe is a way to maintain your perception of events.

Don't worry about trying to "outsmart" the gaslighter: The best way to outsmart a gaslighter is to disengage. You can show up to the discussion with a mountain of evidence, videos, recordings, and more, and a gaslighting person will

---

[3] How to Recognize Gaslighting and Get Help - By Susan York Morris and Crystal Raypole

still find a way to deflect, minimize, or deny. It is more worth it to walk away with your perception intact.[4]

Increase your support system, and share your truth: Sometimes we need external validation from our support system to build our internal confidence, especially when we are victims of being gaslit. You can reduce the psychological and emotional hold that a gaslighter has on you when you share your truths with safe people.[5]

1. **'You're being crazy.'**

Gaslighters will try to manipulate you into questioning your sanity. Making direct comments that undermine your perspective or rationality is a common tactic.

How to respond:

- "Please don't question my ability to think clearly."
- "Even if we don't agree, this is what the reality looks like to me."

2. **'You're overreacting.'**

---

[4] 9 Toxic Phrases 'Gaslighters' Always Use—And How to Respond - Dr. Cortney Warren, Contributor

[5] How To Deal With Gaslighting & Exactly What To Say - Alyssa "Lia" Mancao

By accusing you of being dramatic, the gaslighter attempts to dismiss your concerns as irrational and unfounded.

How to respond:

- "Whether or not you agree with me, this is how I feel right now."
- "I would appreciate it if you didn't judge my feelings. They are mine and not up for debate."

3. **'I was just joking!'**

Gaslighters often downplay their mean-spirited comments or criticism. This can cause you to wonder if you're being overly sensitive, even when you're not.

How to respond:

- "That comment might have been funny to you, but it hurt my feelings."
- "It didn't seem to me like you were joking, and I'd appreciate it if you didn't talk to me that way."

4. **'You made me do it.'**

When something doesn't go as they had planned, gaslighters will often try to avoid taking responsibility by shifting any criticism and blame onto you.

How to respond:

- "I actually can't make you do anything."
- "Your behavior is a reflection of your choices, not mine."

5. **'If you loved me, you'd let me do what I want.'**

When you try to set boundaries with a gaslighter, they may feel wronged and try to make you feel guilty by saying you don't care about them.

How to respond:

- "My boundaries are a reflection of my values and how I choose to live my life."
- "I don't feel comfortable doing this. I am telling, not asking you to respect my boundaries."

6. **'I'm only telling you this because I love you.'**

Gaslighters justify making rude—sometimes abusive—comments by saying they come from a place of love. This can make it harder for you to trust your gut feelings and set healthy boundaries.

How to respond:

- "I appreciate that you love me, but I'm not okay with the way you're talking to me."
- "That's not how I want to be shown love."

7. **'This is all your fault.'**

A gaslighter may try to accuse you of harmful actions, even if there is clear evidence that they are engaging in similar behaviors.

How to respond:

- "I'm sure that I contribute to our relationship struggles in some ways, but so do you. We both have to be willing to change if we want to make this better."
- "I'm willing to take responsibility for my role in this, but I'm not taking responsibility for yours."

8. **'Everyone agrees with me—you're just difficult.'**

By falsely aligning themselves with others, gaslighters may try to manipulate you into believing that you need them. Their goal is to make you think you are alone and that no one else will put up with you.

How to respond:

- "I would appreciate it if you speak for yourself and not for other people."
- "I hear that you find me difficult. Let's stay focused on that."

9. **'The real problem is…'**

When they are called out, gaslighters may try to divert attention away from themselves. This makes it easier to stay focused on what is wrong with someone or something else.

How to respond:

- "Please don't change the subject."
- "It seems like you don't want to acknowledge how you are contributing to the problem."

CHAPTER 13

HOW TO TEACH PEOPLE HOW TO FEEL ABOUT YOU

There is an old saying that first impressions last, and this certainly is the reality when you meet new people. As soon as you meet them, they start forming their own conclusions about you, whether good or bad. Experts say it takes five to fifteen seconds for someone to form their first impression of you. Unfortunately, this first impression takes a long time to change, and most times, you never get a second chance to make a first impression. This first impression can determine whether doors are open or closed for you.

Because this first impression is so important, psychologist Orion Taraban of the YouTube channel PsycHacks says you have to teach people how to feel about you. You have to learn how to present yourself confidently in social relationships. The simplicity of even the way you dress and the way you carry yourself is such an important marker in directing how you should be viewed.

This reminds me of a discussion I had with Michelle, one of my brother's teenage daughters. Michelle felt that men have lost it in the way they present themselves. They have simply stopped grooming themselves. For a few seconds, I started checking my nails and almost visualizing myself standing in front of a mirror and looking at my image from head to toe. Was she cheekily saying that I was also guilty of this? I think I passed, so I confidently continued the discussion with her.

Some of the issues she pointed out as a turnoff were quite surprising to me, as I certainly thought that these were Gen Z or Gen X things that they all embraced as normal, but this was not the case. She was quite critical of the way they dressed with their pants dangling below their waist, how they seemed to lack a visit to the barber, and how their clothing never seemed appropriate for the occasion. She lamented finding a suitable suiter when it came time to select a companion who could follow through to marriage.

Orion Taraban says many things that go into a first impression can be proactively addressed before any interaction. You can give a lot of thought to your appearance, dress, and how you carry yourself in advance; if you do, these will passively exert their influence in any encounter. With this out of the way, you can focus on your tone, expression, body language, and eye contact. This, he proposes, will give the people you are interacting with a positive impression of you. He says you should think of yourself as a vacuum salesman, but instead of a vacuum being the product, you are the product. In the same way, you know all the ins and outs of the vacuum and can confidently highlight your belief that it is the best product available compared to all other vacuum cleaners on the market. This belief is transmitted through all the discussions you have with potential customers as you interact with them to secure a sale. Your business is to present yourself in the best possible light and guide people in the process of making up their minds to form a good and lasting impression of you. Just like with the vacuum salesman, despite your every effort, not everyone will end up buying, and this should not discourage you as the most important people to you are those who see the benefit of you to them and them to you.

Forming a good first impression and presenting yourself with confidence is always a good way to deflate a toxic individual. They will quickly notice this and simply move on to their next potential victim.

Have I not commanded you? Be strong and courageous. Do not be afraid; do not be discouraged, for the Lord your God will be with you wherever you go. (Joshua 1:9 – NIV).

For you created my inmost being; you knit me together in my mother's womb. I praise you because I am fearfully and wonderfully made; your works are wonderful, I know that full well. (Psalm 139:13-14 – NIV).

One thing I have found to be true, and I have seen this in operation many times both personally and while observing people as they interact with others, is that people who dress well make a positive impact on how others perceive them. Don't look like you are going to the office; look like you own the office. You should look like a man of value. This is especially true also for people who work out and are in good physical shape. It seems to be a bonus if they dress well and are also in good shape. It is hard not to respect a person who is in shape because being in shape says so much about them. Just the fact that they are disciplined enough to spend time working out to meet their goal of looking good says something about their character.

Some reasons why people might respect you more when you dress well are:

1. **Shows Self-Respect:** By taking the time to dress well, you are showing respect for yourself, which can earn the respect of others.

2. **Professionalism:** Dressing appropriately for the occasion or setting can convey professionalism and competence.

3. **Confidence:** Well-fitting and stylish clothing can boost your confidence, which can be attractive to others.

4. **Attention to Detail:** Paying attention to your appearance demonstrates that you are detail-oriented and care about how you present yourself.

5. **Respect for Others:** Dressing well for an event or meeting can show respect for the host or others attending.

6. **Social Perception:** People tend to make assumptions about others based on their appearance, so dressing well can positively influence how others perceive you.

7. **Positive First Impressions:** Your clothing is often the first thing people notice about you, so dressing well can help you make a good first impression.

8. **Personal Branding:** Your style can be part of your personal brand, reflecting your personality and values.

9. **Attention and Influence:** Well-dressed individuals often command more attention and may have a greater influence in social or professional settings.

10. **Cultural Norms:** In many cultures, dressing well is a sign of respect for the situation and the people around you, leading to increased respect in return.

There are two other areas I want to highlight when it comes to teaching people how to feel about you. Firstly, wear an infectious smile on your face. This must not be a fake or made-up smile, but a smile birthed from your innermost soul. Secondly, always have an attitude of gratitude. I am always smiling. However, I must confess that in this fast-paced world, I sometimes forget to slow down and say thank you. Sometimes, when you realize this, you have totally lost the opportunity to do it. Truly, first impressions last, and you may never get the second opportunity to say thank you without feeling corny. Yes, I messed up again. So now I am mindful to always slow down to display that attitude of gratitude. I have learned to say "Thank you!" with a big grin on my face.

People will eventually see what is on the inside of you when your true characters start to show. So, outside of forming a good impression on your first interaction, a good recommendation is to make sure the impressions and characters you show on the outside represent the good characters you have on the inside. There is a term called "whitewash sepulcher" that my grandmother often used. This was pulled from the Bible, and she was quick to use it as a guide in almost every situation. This term represents someone who is outwardly professedly virtuous or holy but inwardly corrupted or wicked. It is as if the contents of their hearts are as dead as the contents of a sepulcher.

As water reflects the face, so one's life reflects the heart. (Proverbs 27:19 – NIV).

Not that which goeth into the mouth defileth a man; but that which cometh out of the mouth, this defileth a man. (Matthew 15:11 – KJV).

CHAPTER 14

LET GO, MOVE ON

Toxic people can drain your energy, impact your mental health, and prevent you from achieving your goals. Someone once said that toxic people leave you in a state where you go home and argue with your wife and get angry with your kids. They do this with just one comment.

Despite all the strategic moves you have made, pulling from all the expert advice received that should surely stop them in their tracks, sometimes they don't work out, and you end up instead with more pain and abuse. At that point, you have no choice but to let the toxic person go for your own peace of mind.

Letting go of toxic people can be uncomfortable, but it is ultimately for your own well-being. You deserve to surround yourself with positive, supportive people who uplift you.

Let go of hot coal or you will get burnt!

"Do two walk together, unless they have agreed to meet?" (Amos 3:3 – ESV).

Here are a few tips on how to let go of toxic people:

1. **Identify Toxic Behavior** - Before you can let go of toxic people, you need to identify them first. Look out for people who are always negative, critical or manipulative. They may also be people who always need to be the center of attention or who constantly drain your energy.

2. **Set Boundaries** - Once you have identified toxic behavior, it is important to set boundaries. Let the toxic person know what behavior is unacceptable and what you are willing to tolerate. Stick to these

boundaries, and don't let the toxic person persuade you otherwise.

3. **Distance Yourself** - If the toxic person continues to exhibit toxic behavior, it may be time to distance yourself. This could mean limiting your interactions with them or cutting them off completely.

4. **Seek Support** - Letting go of toxic people can be difficult, so it is important to seek support. Reach out to friends, family or a therapist who can help you through the process.

If toxic people are in your company, you must be doing something that somehow attracts them and explains why they seem comfortable in your company. What are you doing to attract them to you? If you are surrounded by toxic people, there is a part of you that is tolerating (accepting, permitting, condoning, putting up with) them.

If someone is controlling you, it is not their fault; it is yours!

Letting go of toxic people is not always easy, and when doing so, it helps to remember to focus on the next step and not the entire journey. Moving away from negative people takes maturity, self-love, and strong faith. Faith leads to forgiveness, but we also need to keep in mind that forgiveness does not always mean reconnection.

Forgiveness can be a powerful act of letting go and moving forward, even if it doesn't always lead to reconnection with the other person. It is about finding peace within yourself. Forgiving others can help you find peace within yourself. When you forgive someone, you release yourself from the burden of holding on to anger and resentment. By letting go of those negative emotions, you create space for more positivity and inner peace. Forgiveness is a powerful tool that allows you to move forward without being weighed down by past grievances.

All the negative Nancie's can go! Say bye to them!

CHAPTER 15

DEPENDENCY

When I think about dependency, the old saying comes to me, which says, *"Give a man a fish, and you feed him for a day. Teach a man to fish, and you feed him for a lifetime."* This proverb often illustrates the importance of teaching someone how to do something themselves instead of simply doing it for them. Teach them how to be independent instead of dependent on you.

Research done over many years monitoring individuals' lives from childhood to adulthood confirms that children whose parents do everything for them are deprived of the opportunity to develop their problem-solving skills. This leads to low self-esteem when they become adults. This, no doubt, calls to bear the certain long-term negative effects of dependency.

Allowing children to solve daily problems on their own can help boost their self-esteem for several reasons:

1. **Sense of Independence:** When children are allowed to solve problems by themselves, they develop a sense of independence and autonomy. This independence can boost their confidence and help them feel more capable of handling challenges.

2. **Problem-Solving Skills:** By allowing children to tackle daily problems independently, they have the chance to develop and sharpen their problem-solving skills. Successfully resolving issues on their own can be a great confidence-builder and make them feel more capable in their abilities.

3. **Ownership and Responsibility:** When children are allowed to solve their own problems, it gives them a sense of ownership and responsibility over the outcome. This can lead to a feeling of accomplishment and pride when they are able to overcome obstacles by themselves.

The classic dictionary definition for dependency is a situation where you need something or someone and are unable to continue normally without them. Dependency perpetrates the giving of fish as opposed to teaching how to fish.

Let me draw your attention to the term “toxic dependency.” This terminology usually falls outside of the remit of parent and child interaction. Toxic dependency refers to a harmful or unhealthy reliance on someone or something for emotional support, validation, or a sense of identity. It often involves one person becoming excessively reliant on another person in a way that is detrimental to only one of the parties involved. This can lead to a lack of boundaries and an imbalance of power in the relationship.

Toxic dependency speaks to someone who typically perverts the good relationship of one hand washing the other to allow mutual growth but puts a stranglehold over them with the single reason of controlling them and their progress. They typically become the slave to the toxic individual.

Overcoming toxic dependency can be a challenging process, but outside of seeking a therapist, counsellor or support group to help you work through your issues and develop healthier coping mechanisms, you can consider figuring out what situations, emotions or people trigger your dependent behaviors. We need to work on building our self-confidence and self-worth so we are less likely to seek validation from external sources.

CHAPTER 16

TRUST YOUR SIXTH SENSE

Your sixth sense is what someone would call a "gut feeling" or your "inner voice." It is a feeling or intuition of knowing something without the ability to explain it. This intuition can be a valuable tool in decision-making and problem-solving. It often arises from your subconscious mind, where you process information and draw conclusions without being fully aware of it. This can sometimes lead to insights that may help navigate complex situations.

Eric Haseltine, Ph.D. Neuroscientist and the author of "Long Fuse, Big Bang," in speaking about the sixth sense, proposes that there are scientifically valid reasons to trust your feelings and intuitions and that much of what we know, we know without knowing how we know it. I would say this is a spontaneous, impulsive, automatic ability like blinking your eyes.

Another example is when you compare the smiles in two pictures. You know, without thinking why, that one is real and one is fake. Differences such as how much each person's eyes are "smiling" become apparent when you look closely, but how did you know that crinkling around the eyes conveys genuine happiness, while the absence of such crinkling means a person is faking it?

Similarly, if you were sitting in a noisy restaurant with your eyes closed and someone walked by you close to your left side, you would somehow sense their presence even if they made no sound.

Bestselling British author, David Gemmell, in his book *Troy #3: Fall of Kings*, puts it like this, *"Trust your instincts and make judgments on what your heart tells you. The heart will not betray you."* I agree with this sentiment, as this is the feeling that makes you feel like something is not right. It is that voice in your head that makes you know what is right and wrong.

I am convinced without a doubt that we all possess a sixth sense; a kind of premonition when things don't appear as they seem. It is as if, at these times, God gives us a glimpse into the future with a strong urgency to act in our own defence. How many times have we felt that need to travel a different route from the one we were used to taking on a daily commute? How many times have we felt the sense to pass up on using that one automated teller machine that seems more convenient for another that is outside your route but seems more secure? We may not know for sure what catastrophe we missed by giving credence to that feeling, but deep inside, we feel a sense of satisfaction that the other choice would have born disaster. These are telling signs of that sixth sense. This sixth sense is not something considered to be rational but mainly intuitive. It is based on what you feel to be true without conscious reasoning.

Trust your sixth sense!

When we get these feelings indicating character flaws in individuals, let us treat them as a red flag signalling impending danger. What lies waiting inside their heads is not visible, so we have to learn how to trust our senses early and establish boundaries to restrict their further advances.

It is important to remember that even though our intuitions can be so valuable, they are not infallible and should be used in conjunction with evidence-based reasoning. Sometimes, when someone is emotionally unsafe for you, there can be physical manifestations that signal they are unsafe to be around. We should also be on the lookout for these indicators. Sometimes, our gut feelings can be influenced by biases or past experiences, and it is helpful to consider all the available information before making a final decision.

CHAPTER 17

BE CAREFUL WHO YOU SHARE GOOD NEWS WITH

There are some people I call the vision killers. These individuals are not happy with the progress of others and will use the negative outcome and the bad situations they have encountered to offer you advice. These persons never seem to have a win to speak about or a clear vision of an accomplishment they hope for.

These vision killers have to be avoided, and no decision should be made, nor should action be taken as a result of their council. Just like a ship without a rudder, they have no clear direction and float around aimlessly without reaching a final destination.

Where there is no vision, the people perish: (Proverbs 29:18a – KJV).

I remember a true story told by a mother. Let's call her Jeniffer. Jeniffer had a menial job at a very profitable conglomerate company and had put in an application for her son at a very prestigious university. Jeniffer's son, in my mind, was an absolute genius who had overcome all the obstacles he had faced so far with distinction. With a level of satisfaction and feeling overwhelmed with joy at her son's success, she decided to share this good fortune with one of the senior executives. The executive's immediate response was that her son would not get accepted as his child had also applied to that same university in the past but was not accepted.

This could have been interpreted in many ways, but I conclude that no matter how you spin it, the final result is that all of them indicate a financial bias. This was a comparison of financial status. With all the wealth he had, and his child not being accepted, then certainly Jeniffer's child would also not be accepted.

Jeniffer possessed a determined personality, and this interaction with the executive did not daunt her. In the end, her son did get accepted to the university. He was able to complete his program of study in five years. He is now gainfully employed and receiving the financial benefits of his academic success.

We must learn how to filter what comes to us by way of advice. People will offer advice out of goodwill, but poor advice is simply poor advice.

If any of you lacks wisdom, you should ask God, who gives generously to all without finding fault, and it will be given to you. (James 1:5 – NIV).

Even while being careful with whom we share our good news with and as we weigh out the advice we receive, we also have to be aware that having good friends and friendships is important to us. There is an old saying that good friends are better than pocket money, which speaks of the security and assurance good friends give you. The people you choose as your good friends are the people who will be happy for you when good things happen to you, people who will celebrate your opportunities as if it is their own, who will tell you what you need to hear even if it hurts, who will smile when you smile, and are most likely to shed a tear when you go through your sad seasons.

It can be very difficult when we try to do life on our own. Humans are social beings and we depend on each other for our entire ecosystem to work. If we were all hands, then how would we walk? If we were all feet, then how would we talk? This ecosystem is reminiscent of our body, which is joined and fitted together and acts together in unity and purpose. Imagine if we were all hairdressers, then who would do the cooking or who would farm the land? Life works out much better when we have a team of good supporters around us to encourage us on the way. It is said that teamwork makes the dream work, and this certainly holds true most of the time.

Surround yourself with people who make you better!

I recently saw a cartoon showing a tiny dragon sitting on the back of a big panda. The dragon asked the panda, *"Which is more important; the journey or the destination?"* The panda replied, *"The company."* We need to enjoy the company of good friends more than the journey to achieve our life goals or the destination we reach when we achieve these goals. If we learn to enjoy the company and learn from those around us, our lives may be more enriched and fulfilling.

This cartoon gave me an added perspective on how I accepted things before. Previously, I stuck to what Earl Nightingale said about success in his book *The Strangest Secret*. In this book, he defined success as the progressive realization of a worthy goal. The key is the progressive realization of a goal. But I am now adding that the progressing realization of a goal while we enjoy the company of good friends who help us achieve those goals. These are the persons you are pouring into that are also pouring into you.

Wholeheartedly celebrate the success of others!

You can often determine if the persons around you—in your circle of friends—are the good friends and supporters you need or if your relationship with them is one-sided. You are always the one lifting their hands in support, but they are never available to steady your hands when they grow tired. Psychologists believe that people with three to five people in their friend group are happiest and most satisfied with their lives. Other studies agree that no matter how many friends you have in general, only the five closest people matter to you.

Iron sharpeneth iron; so a man sharpeneth the countenance of his friend. (Proverbs 27:17 – KJV).

CHAPTER 18

CHANGE IS POSSIBLE

I believe all persons can change; call it redemption or something like that or whatever you choose to call it. As long as we breathe this breath of life, everyone and anyone has an opportunity to change. The only caveat to this, however, is if they want to change. People don't like to change, even if the change will be beneficial to them. We are creatures of habit, and once we are settled on a routine, it can be almost impossible for us to act outside of it. Look at people in church for example who will sit in the same seat every Sunday for as long as they are going to that church. If they move to another church, it is the same: find a seat and that is it every Sunday.

Andrew Bustamante is a former CIA intelligence officer, US Air Force Graduate, and successful Fortune 10 corporate advisor. Andrew says that based on his training, people sometimes develop a catastrophic thinking mindset where they think of the worst possible outcome of a situation, and then they become fixated on this position until they start living out that outcome, forgetting that there can be many other outcomes, some of which may not be detrimental as what we are thinking. I agree with Andrew and will add that we are not to be too hasty to write off people. We sometimes need to think of how we would have liked others to treat us if the roles were somehow switched and we were in the position of the person who needed help. It is not doing unto others as they have done to you but treating others the same way you would like to be treated. Certainly, we would not want them to have such catastrophic thoughts of us. We can't turn back the hand of time. What has been done in the past is done, and we certainly don't have any control over it. However, what we have control of is the future, and we can choose how we move forward.

Change equals opportunity!

Let us be available and ready to say, "I will help you." I am not saying we are to be naive and put ourselves in harms way, but as long as the person accepts and sees the need for change, then let us offer to help them in whatever ways we can. Help does not mean we take the person under total keep and care. Remember, help can be as small as finding the person who is trained to help them through their transition and making the first call to secure an appointment for them to see the expert or offering to take them to or pick them up after their first meeting.

LOVE is a verb; it is a word of action, and we cannot say we love someone, want to see the best for them, and are not willing to prove that love with our actions.

Love is a word of action!

The reality of life is that people will change if they want to change, and this is also true of toxic people. For the person showing the love and willingness to assist someone to change, their assistance does not somehow compel the person to change. They don't change by you telling them. It is therefore not important that the toxic persons only say they will change or that they want to change, but instead they should back up their words with actions by movement in the direction of change. For example, they should not say, "I am going to therapy," but instead, they should say, "I am in therapy." This is taking actions required for change to happen. No amount of self-pity, penitent speech or saying sorry by them will move the needle if they have not taken action. They have to take action. They have to take that first step.

The most important step anyone can take is the first step. There are some people, however, who believe the second step is more important than the first step as the second step shows and builds consistency, but, as for me, I stick to my point that the first is the most important step because you can't take a second step without first taking a first step.

Change is about taking action!

When it comes to toxic people, a sad reality is that they often think they don't need to change and that the other person is always the person who needs changing. This further reinforces the thought that you have to stand by and only be ready to assist, if they have already committed to change and take action to change.

CHAPTER 19

EIGHT SIGNS SOMEONE IS GOOD FOR YOU, NOT TOXIC

To be clear, this is not a complete or final list of how to know someone is toxic. However, this list is intended to offer a few points so you can quickly assess your interactions with others. With this, you can take action sooner rather than later. Your natural instinct would have told you to draw closer to people who are good for you and create distance between those who are not good for you.

1. **They support your dreams and aspirations:** A sign that someone is good for you is that they genuinely support and encourage your goals, dreams, and ambitions. They are there to uplift and motivate you rather than holding you back or downplaying your aspirations.

2. **They communicate effectively:** Effective communication is a crucial aspect of any healthy relationship. A good partner listens actively, expresses their thoughts and feelings honestly, and resolves conflicts in a respectful manner. They make you feel heard, understood, and valued.

3. **They respect your boundaries:** Someone who is good for you respects your personal boundaries and tries not to push you beyond what you are comfortable with. They understand that boundaries are necessary for self-care and overall well-being and try to ensure that they are being considerate of your limits.

4. **They show empathy and compassion:** A person who is good for you exhibits empathy and compassion towards your feelings and experiences. They try to understand your perspective, offer emotional support when needed, and are willing to

put themselves in your shoes to better navigate difficult situations.

5. **They encourage personal growth:** Healthy relationships involve personal growth and development. A good partner supports your personal growth and encourages you to be the best version of yourself. They inspire you to explore new interests, learn new things, and challenge yourself rather than holding you back or being intimidated by your growth.

6. **They prioritize your well-being:** A person who is good for you genuinely cares about your overall well-being. They express concern for your physical and emotional health, encourage self-care, and are willing to help and support you through difficult times. They prioritize your happiness and work towards maintaining a balanced and healthy relationship.

7. **They show trust and reliability:** Trust is a fundamental element of any strong relationship. A good partner is reliable, consistent, and can be counted on. They keep their promises, are honest with you, and consistently demonstrate trustworthiness. They create a sense of security in the relationship, allowing you to have confidence and faith in their intentions and actions.

8. **They bring out the best in you:** One of the strongest signs that someone is good for you is that they bring out the best in you. They inspire you to be a better person, to grow, and to pursue your passions. They provide support, encouragement, and a safe space for you to be yourself. They bring joy, positivity, and a sense of fulfillment to your life.

You can expect that the people who are generally bad for you would do and act in a matter that is totally opposite to the actions listed above.

Hear with your ears, but listen with your eyes!

It is not just about what people say but also what they do. A simple example is when you and your partner are sitting at home taking a break from the hustle and bustle of the work world. You are in the middle of watching your favorite TV program when your partner spark up a conversation. In the middle of them speaking, you hear them saying *"But, honey, you're not listening to me."* Your ears, which is the tool for hearing, are open to what they are saying, but your eyes are glued to the TV. Active listening means your ears should be hearing, but your eyes should also be looking at the person who is the source of the communication. This is even more important when the person wanting to have a conversation with you is the one you care about and love. That person should get your one hundred percent attention when it is needed.

CHAPTER 20

PEOPLE WHO TALK BEHIND YOUR BACK—THE SILENT ASSASSINS

Michelle, a good friend of mine, refers to people who talk behind your back as silent assassins. This is like a code phrase used by her when she wants to draw your attention to the actions of someone without the crowd recognizing the true meaning of what is being said.

People who talk behind your back are the silent assassins—backstabbers! Call them what name you want to; they too fall into the realm of toxic characters. The iconic American R&B group from Canton, Ohio, formed in 1958 called the O'Jays could not have said it better in their song aptly titled "Back Stabbers." I encourage you to take a few minutes and search for this song online and have a listen to it in its entirety. Not only will it make a good listen, but it will help you to zone in on the thoughts I am sharing in this chapter.

The backstabber, or as Michelle puts it, the silent assassin, says one thing to your face, like showing concern for you, but tells others something totally different. In other words, the silent assassins will spread rumors and lie about you to make you look bad. You think of this person as a friend or confidant, but they are not trustworthy at all. In the case of the O'Jays, their song zoomed in on that friend who tries to court your woman behind your back while pretending to be a good friend when they are in your company. This is such a betrayal of your trust. It is no wonder you need to place yourself beyond the reach of these people.

You may have realized a similarity between the silent assassins and persons who gossip. Both characters employ similar methods.

Some folks say they're friends. Well, news flash; they're not!

In the workplace, gossip and backstabbing can create a toxic work culture, decrease productivity, and harm relationships with colleagues and supervisors. This can result in missed opportunities for growth and promotions or even lead to job loss.

CHAPTER 21

THE MAN IN THE MIRROR

Let me draw your attention to two quotes. One says: *"We all have monsters,"* and the other says: *"Whoever fights monsters should see to it that in the process, he does not become a monster."* These monsters I am referring to represent deeply hidden aspects of ourselves that we try our endeavor best not to expose to others. As humans, we can sometimes be so conceited, thinking it is never us and always the other person.

In 1979, Nobel Prize-winning economist Milton Friedman was interviewed on the Phil Donahue Show. Donahue confronted Friedman on greed and the free market system. Freedman's reply was to challenge Donahue to name one society that does not work on greed. Freedman even went on to say in a cynical manner that, of course, none of us are greedy and that the other person is always greedy.

It would be nice to exclude ourselves from being toxic with a sense that *"I am better than everyone"* and with some sort of badge of honor on your chest, saying, *"Follow me! Follow me! I am the model of righteousness."* Even in this state, you have found yourself wanting. Romans 3:23 declares, *"For all have sinned, and come short of the glory of God." (KJV)*. The mere fact that you are a human, as we all are, and on our individual journey of discovery, shows that we are constantly on a path of learning and transformation, and the reality is, this will be the case until we leave this earth.

Don't be the toxic person you hate!

I have been involved in various aspects of mathematics at every stage of my academic development, from primary school to university, and have constantly excelled. Actually, mathematics was my major for my university degree. I have concluded that I am a critical thinker who tends to analyze absolutely everything. Let's just say I like to make sense of things. Sometimes, however, I think maybe I am an overthinker. Overthinking is a common trait among many individuals, and it often goes hand in hand with being analytical and detail-oriented. Overthinkers have a tendency to analyze every detail of a situation or problem. They scrutinize various possibilities, potential outcomes, and potential risks, which can lead to thorough analysis but also prolonged decision-making processes. One of the defining characteristics of overthinkers is their ability to anticipate future scenarios. They are adept at considering multiple outcomes and preparing for different possibilities, which can be both a strength and a source of anxiety.

Here is a little humor on thinkers: When a thinker says they love you, believe them because they have already gone through all the many reasons not to love you.

Critical thinkers will question everything until they understand!

Reaching this point of self-acceptance was never easy. I have had to drag myself from the edge of despair many times, even from the point of questioning my sanity. I wanted so much to find out if making sense of things was normal behavior for a normal individual. This was a tough path to entertain, but happily, in the end, my research pointed to the fact that being a thinker is quite normal for persons who gravitate towards complex disciplines such as physics, engineering, and mathematics. These persons tend to be critical thinkers, and it is standard for us to see multiple perspectives. I saw in an interview with this guy who admits to being a deep thinker who says he has counted down to the number of buttons used in the construction of a designer sofa in a room he was in while waiting for the interview to begin. I can definitely understand this type of behavior as I have used a sequencing principle many times.

An important observation on thinkers is that they have to take control of their thinking and be careful not to allow themselves to continue into a spiral of unending loops, often leading to no final conclusion. We must also watch out for statements we make like, *"This is how I am," "I'm no-nonsense," "I don't fear anything," "I'm a survivor," "I do what I have to do," "Either you fit in, or you get passed by," "You can't influence me; it's my way or the highway."* While these work well for you as an individual, we need to be careful not to project them on others as we use these statements to influence or control them in some way, mainly through fear.

As it relates to controlling your thoughts, I like how Napoleon Hill puts it. He says: *"Self-discipline begins with the mastery of your thoughts. If you don't control what you think, you can't control what you do. Simply, self-discipline enables you to think first and act afterward."* What a wonderful insight this is, and I encourage all thinkers, overthinkers, and anyone who has an inkling that they lack self-control to find some wisdom in those words.

Step back and look at yourself!

It is essential to recognize when we are feeling emotionally charged and take steps to manage those emotions. We cannot see our reflection in boiling water, and so it is when you have to make a decision and emotions exist that confuse us and hinder us from making a decision based on reason and logic. When this happens, you have to take stock of what is happening inside you and perhaps seek a quiet place where you can think clearly and objectively as you examine what is true and what is false.

Our emotional states can significantly impact how we behave toward others, and this makes the difference if we operate as toxic individuals or operate relaxed and comfortable in ourselves. We have to learn to find our way in life as we interact with toxic people and be careful not to become toxic ourselves. It is easy for toxic people to suck us into their toxicity.

Know your triggers and watch out for the tactics used by toxic individuals to activate those triggers!

By learning how to regulate our emotions, we can reduce the likelihood of engaging in toxic behaviors and build healthier relationships with those around us. This can be considered a way of positively and constructively using your toxicity.

Stand fast therefore in the liberty wherewith Christ hath made us free, and be not entangled again with the yoke of bondage. (Galatians 5:1 – KJV).

CHAPTER 22

TRUE IDENTITY

My final observation is that the sooner you realize that only you can make yourself happy, the sooner you will learn the greatest lesson. There is a saying that I heard, but I am not sure of its source. It says, *"True happiness is internal. It's in your head and heart."* When you go out, you should take happiness to the people and not expect happiness from them. This is also true when we go to work. Oftentimes, we have an underlying expectation that we will get happiness from work as truly this is the place that gives us an accreditation of value to the worth we have in society.

Certain professions may be deemed more prestigious or important based on their impact on society, the level of skill required or financial compensation. This can lead individuals to equate their self-worth with the perceived status of their job. It is important to remember that a person's value extends far beyond their occupation and everyone has unique qualities and contributions to make, regardless of their job title. The recommendation even then is that we should be taking “happy” to work with us and not expect to receive happiness from work.

We should not rely on others to define, satisfy, fulfill or validate our identity. If we lose our identity, we also lose our character, which ultimately means we have lost everything. Our character is important to God, and that is why He instructs us to walk by the leading of His Spirit so the actions of our flesh are replaced with God’s attributes. We can lose other stuff without an issue, but not our identity. Identity refers to our sense of who we are as individuals, and as members of the various social groups we are a part of.

Being yourself can sometimes feel a bit weird or uncomfortable, and this is because we have not spent enough time understanding and appreciating the unique individual we are, so we seek validation outside of ourselves. This can lead to a lack of confidence, and then we are open to the schemes of a toxic person whose ultimate wish is to drain every ounce of our energy. We should have the confidence and self-awareness necessary to just shrug them off. With that, they will move to the next host.

You may be asking, “Where does the source of my true identity come from? What gives me true happiness on the inside?” I believe our identity is in Jesus Christ. I have included a few verses below that confirm this belief.

We are made in the image of God!

So you are no longer a slave, but God's child; and since you are his child, God has made you also an heir. (Galatians 4:7 – NIV).

But you are a chosen people, a royal priesthood, a holy nation, God's special possession, that you may declare the praises of him who called you out of darkness into his wonderful light. (1 Peter 2:9 – NIV).

For we are His workmanship, created in Christ Jesus for good works, which God prepared beforehand that we should walk in them. (Ephesians 2:10 – NKJV).

Walk in the Word!

You're blessed when you stay on course, walking steadily on the road revealed by God. You're blessed when you follow his directions, doing your best to find him. That's right—you don't go off on your own; you walk straight along the road he set. You, God, prescribed the right way to live; now you expect us to live it. Oh, that my steps might be steady, keeping to the course you set; Then I'd never have any regrets in comparing my life with your counsel. I thank you for speaking straight from your heart; I learn the pattern of your righteous ways. I'm going to do what you tell me to do; don't ever walk off and leave me. (Psalm 119:1-8 – The Message)

Be he transformed by the renewing of your mind!

Do not conform to the pattern of this world, but be transformed by the renewing of your mind. Then you will be able to test and approve what God's will is—his good, pleasing and perfect will. (Romans 12:2 – NIV).

I am mindful that not everyone will agree with me on the source of our true identity, and it is not my intention to have conflict about this with anyone. However, I am affirming that we all need to find our purpose for our existence and allow this to be the guiding principle that governs us. Let this true identity be our center or north star, as some call it. This center brings a sense of clarity, determination, and meaning to life. When someone aligns their actions, values, and goals with their true identity, they experience greater fulfillment and satisfaction.

Your center causes you to understand how to recognize truth!

Whether we are a toxic person or the person who falls prey to toxic people, the reality is, it is time to audit and moderate yourself. If you are toxic, by now, you will have realized the hurt you cause others and should be convinced that you need to change. If you are the person who receives hurt from toxic persons by now, you would have realized that you can, need, and should be free. Find that freedom today. It is time to let go, thrive, and find the emotional freedom you deserve.

CHAPTER 23

PLEASE LEAVE A REVIEW

HELLO THERE!

If you have read this far in my book, it means you have learned some new skills that equipped you to move and find freedom from toxic people.

I humbly ask that you leave an honest review of my book on your Amazon portal. Early reviews are the single most important factor in determining if a book succeeds, so I'm incredibly thankful for people, like you, who I can rely on to leave one.

Reviews can be 1-2 sentences and should take about 30 seconds to leave *(and would make a huge difference for me)*. Thanks so much for your support. I deeply appreciate it.

Best,
Zeelah S. Davis

www.ingramcontent.com/pod-product-compliance
Lightning Source LLC
LaVergne TN
LVHW051136080426
835510LV00018B/2444

* 9 7 8 1 9 5 8 4 0 4 7 9 9 *